LOST LINES OF WALES
MONMOUTHSHIRE EASTERN VALLEY

GEOFFREY LLOYD

CONTENTS

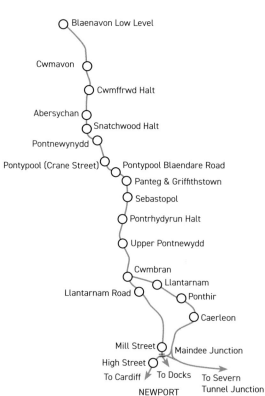

Blaenavon Low Level
Cwmavon
Cwmffrwd Halt
Abersychan
Snatchwood Halt
Pontnewynydd
Pontypool (Crane Street)
Pontypool Blaendare Road
Panteg & Griffithstown
Sebastopol
Pontrhydyrun Halt
Upper Pontnewydd
Cwmbran
Llantarnam
Llantarnam Road
Ponthir
Caerleon
Mill Street
Maindee Junction
High Street
To Cardiff
To Docks
To Severn Tunnel Junction
NEWPORT

FOREWORD

This series of books aims to revive nostalgic memories of some of the more interesting and scenic railways that served the people of Wales. This volume recalls the line that ran from Blaenavon at the head of the eastern valley of Monmouthshire, sometimes referred to as the Llywd Valley, through to Newport and its docks in the south.

In common with many of the south Wales valley routes, this line followed a river course, in this case the Afon Llwyd or 'grey river', so named as it was once used as a coal washery for the pits in the north around Blaenavon. *Bradshaw's Descriptive Railway Hand-Book of Great Britain and Ireland 1861* described the area as 'districts rich in mineral products, but not of essential importance to the general tourist.'

The line carried a considerable volume of traffic from the time it first opened. The availability of the Maindee East Loop coupled with the opening of the Severn Tunnel in 1886 vastly simplified the transfer of coal traffic to London, Portland and Southampton where bunkering Royal Navy and ocean-going commercial shipping was experiencing considerable growth. Through passenger trains from Plymouth to Manchester could also use this loop thus avoiding the need for a stop and a reversal at Newport. They continued north through Pontypool Road, their first stop since leaving Bristol, to serve Hereford, Shrewsbury and Birkenhead on tracks controlled solely or jointly by the Great Western Railway.

Passenger traffic could be especially busy throughout the summer months with many day trippers travelling to the resorts of Barry Island and Porthcawl. At Newport, connections were available to Cardiff, Bristol, Birmingham, London and many other destinations.

The Eastern Valley line closed to passenger traffic from 30th April 1962 although freight continued until 1980 ending with the closure of the Big Pit Mine at Blaenavon. The last return passenger train from Newport to Blaenavon actually ran on Sunday 29th April 1962.

The line from Newport to Hereford, known originally as the north and west route and now referred to as the Welsh Marches Line, provides frequent services to Shrewsbury and beyond.

The line is still heavily used for freight traffic through Caerleon, whose station buildings and yard remain largely intact in private ownership. The station sites at Ponthir and Llantarnam have long since disappeared and there is no evidence now of the line branching to the left towards Pontypool and Blaenavon at Llantarnam Junction.

However, part of the old line north of Pontypool is now a cycleway and some effort has been made to identify former station sites such as Snatchwood Halt, so one can still walk or cycle on this part of the route and imagine what it was like in its operational days.

INTRODUCTION

This railway line running 16 miles due north from Newport to Blaenavon was built to capitalise on the growing industrial base in the area and to bring passengers to the important town of Newport and freight to its docks. The industrial history of this part of Wales can be traced back to as early as 1425 when there is a record of iron smelting at Pontypool. Richard Hanbury built the first ironworks here in 1577 and the first tinplate to be produced in the UK was made here when a method of rolling iron was introduced by John Hanbury in 1865.

Towards the end of the eighteenth century, a consortium of wealthy coal-owners and industrialists sought to construct canals and wagon ways in the valleys of Monmouthshire to transport goods to Newport. The first Canal Acts of 1759 and 1760 were private not parliamentarian. Parliament used Private Acts, so called because they conferred powers or benefits on specific individuals or bodies rather than the general public in order to authorise new canal routes. Incorporated by Act of Parliament on 3rd June 1792 'The Company of Proprietors of the Monmouthshire Canal Navigation' came into existence. This Act gave it authority to build canals

and tramroads and to link them with quarries, iron works and coal mines within an eight mile radius of the canal and further allowed anyone who owned such a business to request that a tram road or wagon road be built to link their business to the canal. If the canal company did not agree to such a request within three months, the applicant could build a route at their own expense and without the consent of the owners of the lands or rivers that the route crossed.

The Company was authorised to build two eleven mile long canals, one in the eastern valley and the other in the western valley of Monmouthshire. The canal in the eastern valley was to run from Pontnewynydd to Newport where it joined the river Usk. This was finally opened in 1796. The prize was Newport with its docks, wharves and position on the banks of the Severn Estuary and access to the global markets that lay beyond its shores as iron and coal exports were expanding rapidly. There were already tramways beyond Pontnewynydd, which brought mineral products to the canal where they had to be loaded onto barges for onward conveyance to Newport.

One of the first horse drawn tramroads in Monmouthshire was the Caerleon tramroad built in 1793 by Nicholas Blannin who used it to link the forge he rented at Caerleon to Ponthir tin works and then on to join the canal south of Cwmbran. This was built at his own cost when the Monmouthshire Canal Company refused to do so.

Although the Company was quite prosperous and paid good dividends to shareholders, this was at the expense of neglecting the maintenance of their tram roads. The high costs being charged for their use prompted some shippers to propose building their own railways and in 1842 a group of disgruntled traders, who complained about the length of time it took for barges to travel along the canal from Pontnewynydd to Newport and the expense involved, announced they would build their own railway. This was to be called the Newport and Nantyglo Railway, beginning near the Town Dock and travelling north up a steep incline towards High Cross crossing to Cwmbran and Pontnewynydd back to Blaina and finally terminating at the Nantyglo Ironworks, a total distance of some 21 miles. This proposal was at the zenith of the so-called 'railway mania' when no less

than 272 Acts of Parliament were passed authorising new railway schemes. Although the project seemed to have the backing of several influential people this was an ambitious and expensive undertaking and eventually the project was abandoned. Whether this was just a veiled threat to the MCC or a real proposal is questionable, but it seemed to have the desired effect!

The very idea of a rival company was anathema to the MCC so in order to neutralise this threat to their profitability, they sought powers to build their own line to Newport. In July 1845 the MCC received Parliamentary approval for an Act to build a railway from Newport to Pontypool. An Act of 13th August 1846 stated that this railway had not yet been made and provided for certain branch railways to be connected with it and for incorporation of a new company to be called the Monmouthshire Railway Company known affectionately as the Mice, Rats & Cats line. Power was given for this new company to purchase the MCC but this was not exercised, although certain provisions of the Act were amended and extended and the name was changed to the Monmouthshire Railway and Canal Company. Soon afterwards, the MRCC surveyed the whole of the canal with a view to draining it and building a railway in its place.

At about the same time the Newport, Abergavenny & Hereford Railway had a Bill before Parliament to build a standard gauge line to link those towns. However Parliament was concerned to restrict what it saw as unnecessary parallel routes and in authorising the NA&HR line in 1846 refused permission for a line south of Pontypool. The NA&HR had to make a junction with the MRCC and use its line from Pontypool to Newport.

At the time of authorisation there was a national financial crisis and it proved difficult to raise the required capital for construction, which delayed the project. The first section of the Eastern Valley line was eventually opened on 30th June 1852. The NA&HR was opened to goods traffic on 30th July 1852 and to passenger services on 2nd January 1854.

The MRCC began its passenger services to Pontypool from a temporary terminus in Newport at Marshes Turnpike Gate, in August 1852. No booking facilities were available at the station and passengers had to buy their tickets at the Lock Office in High Street, which was a good ten minutes walk away although a bus was made available. The opening of the station was a grand affair with great pomp and ceremony accompanied by the cannons and band of the 48th (Northamptonshire) Regiment of Foot. There were six stations between Pontypool and Newport and the line was extended southwards to a new terminus at Mill Street in March 1853 when the temporary station at Marshes Turnpike Gate was closed. The line north from Pontypool to Blaenavon was opened in October 1854 with double track provided as far as Cwmffrwd Halt.

The MRCC was not noted for the smooth running of its trains due to insufficient investment in their infrastructure. This was demonstrated on Friday 3rd July 1863 when an express train travelling from the West Midlands to Newport was involved in a derailment at Cwmbran. According to local newspapers, two farmers walking nearby witnessed the accident and in their statement said that the driver and fireman jumped off the engine when it left the rails. The train hit the platform of the new station where a painter was thrown off his ladder and broke his leg. The carriage directly behind the locomotive hit and mounted the platform with debris flying everywhere as the engine rebounded, fell onto its right side and still in motion carried on travelling for some distance. The carriages fell over each other whilst the rails were ripped apart with one rail penetrating the boiler. There were a number of serious injuries and unfortunately the driver, Robert M'ghee, was killed outright.

A more unusual accident occurred in the early hours of the morning of Sunday 12th November 1871 when a runaway engine coupled to a brake van travelled all the way from Pontypool Road station to Newport demolishing no less that fifteen level-crossing gates as well as causing serious damage to signal posts, telegraph posts and even signal boxes. After clearing an innumerable number of points, the runaway engine was brought to a standstill by the brake van leaving the line a short distance beyond Waterloo Junction, where it ran into an embankment causing considerable damage to the van but little damage to the engine, which was back in service the following day. Fortunately, at that time of the morning, there were few pedestrians about and nobody seemed to have been injured in this bizarre episode.

Although the tramroads in Monmouthshire were extensive they were quite isolated from the rest of Great Britain. Not until 18th June 1850 did a main line reach Newport when the South Wales Railway opened a broad gauge line between Cheltenham and Swansea. The arrival of the first train carried many dignitaries including architect and engineer Isambard Kingdom Brunel. However, the SWR could best be described as an east-west axis line and envisaged no direct connections with any other company at the time. It was amalgamated with the GWR in 1863 and the track converted from broad to standard gauge in 1873.

The MRCC line prospered for around 20 years until the opening of the Pontypool, Caerleon & Newport Railway which was backed by the GWR, on 17th September 1874, which created a parallel route from Newport to Pontypool. Acknowledging that the GWR now had the upper hand the MRCC granted it running rights over its entire network from 1st August 1875. In 1877 the GWR invited tenders for the building of stations at Cwmbran, Ponthir and Pontygarnedd or Pontycarna, although it appears that these were different spellings for the same location and ultimately no station with these names was built. However new stations were opened at Caerleon, Ponthir, Llantarnam and Cwmbran on the PCN line. In April 1878 a short connecting branch was opened between Llantarnam Junction and Cwmbran Junction on the MRCC and on 1st August 1880 a new station at Cwmbran was opened. All passenger trains were then routed via Caerleon to Newport High Street, which was completely rebuilt and enlarged to receive the new traffic and opened on 11th March 1880. Closure of Mill Street station then followed with the original MRCC line being used for freight only.

Mill Street Yard continued to operate for goods and freight from the Eastern Valley through to Newport docks until 27th October 1963 when the line was severed at Oakfield sidings, Cwmbran. The remaining section of the line closed on 28th November 1966.

Newport continued to grow and prosper in the nineteenth century and the first decades of the twentieth. The primary means of land transport was by rail and the dominant traffic flow was coal for export or coastal shipping. A huge area of railway sidings was established to serve the docks and a considerable volume of loaded wagons were held awaiting the availability of a ship for onward transit. By 1908 there were over 100 miles of railway sidings at Newport docks and in addition there were transit sheds accommodating goods that required undercover storage. The method of loading coal was by hoists, which lifted the loaded railway wagons from ground level in order to tip their contents into the ships' holds.

Following the outbreak of World War One in 1914 and for the period immediately afterwards, the GWR and all other railway companies throughout the land, which totalled approximately 120, were brought under government control for the duration of the conflict. There was little effect on passenger services for the first two years and freight workings were mainly for the transportation of coal from the south Wales coalfields. As well as serving the ports within the GWR network, large quantities of Welsh coal were conveyed northwards to Grangemouth on the Firth of Forth. Here it was finally loaded onto colliers for the Grand Fleet at Scapa Flow. These coal trains became known as 'Jellicoe Specials' named after Admiral of the Fleet, Lord Jellicoe.

After the Great War, the Railways Act of 1921 enforced the amalgamation of Britain's many independent railway companies into four large groups. This grouping took place in 1923 and the 'Big Four' remained in existence until 1947 when the railways were nationalised under the Transport Act 1947. British Railways came into existence as the business name of the Railway Executive of the British Transport Commission on 1st January 1948. BR was divided into regions, which were initially based on the areas controlled by the former Big Four.

The Railway Executive was conscious that some lines on the network were unprofitable and a programme of closures began almost immediately after nationalisation. The Executive was abolished in 1953 by the Conservative government and control of BR transferred to the parent BTC and other changes

were made including the return of road haulage to the private sector. By the middle of the decade it was clear that BR was in trouble particularly in the freight haulage business where they were losing ground to road traffic. The general financial position of BR worsened until an operating loss was recorded in 1955.

Published in December 1954 a review, known as *Modernisation and Re-Equipment of the British Railways*, was ordered by the government in order to bring the railways up to date and help eliminate their financial deficit by 1962. This review became known as the 'Modernisation Plan' and led to a government White Paper being produced in 1956. The aim was to increase speed, reliability, safety and line capacity through a series of measures, which would make services more attractive to passengers and freight operators thus recovering traffic that was being lost to the roads.

Attempts were made to increase passenger revenue on unprofitable lines and the introduction of the Derby built three car Diesel Multiple Units in 1957 to the Eastern and Western Valley lines provided for a cleaner and more comfortable service, and passenger numbers did indeed improve slightly as a result. Unfortunately timetable amendments to the advertised services that were introduced made travel unattractive for connections at Newport for important destinations such as London, Bristol and Birmingham. As a consequence of these changes passenger numbers declined resulting in continuing financial losses. These losses combined with the planned building of Llanwern steelworks to the east of Newport in the 1960s led to the announcement of the withdrawal of local services. It was alleged that freight trains running to the new steelworks would be disrupted by the local passenger services. However, as valley line trains used tracks not connected with the through running lines at Newport. BR management used this as an excuse to withdraw the loss making passenger services on both the Eastern and the Western valley lines.

As an example of timetable amendments, the 7.05am service from Blaenavon was scheduled to arrive at Newport at 7.59am, just in time to connect with the prestigious 8.08am *South Wales Pullman* non-stop service to London (Paddington). Similarly, the 4.25pm service from Blaenavon, due to arrive at Newport at 5.16pm, connected with *The Pembroke Coast Express* through service to Paddington, which departed at 5.20pm. It can clearly be seen that these timings are somewhat 'tight'. In reality trains were being held at signals for a few minutes, whether deliberately or not, such that vitally important connections were lost, which only added to the unattractiveness of the service.

The only service that ensured reasonable connection times to direct named trains to London was the 9.00am from Blaenavon scheduled to arrive Newport at 9.54am and gave ample time to connect with *The Red Dragon* non-stop service that left Newport at 10.20am and arrived at Paddington at 12.55.

The first northbound departure from Newport to Blaenavon was at 4.45am. This was predominantly a workmen's train and special cheap tickets were available. The first southbound train from Blaenavon departed at 5.05am but went only as far as Cwmbran and was mostly used by workers travelling to factories such as Girling.

Service frequency showed 18 trains a day in each direction until closure of the line but connections with main line services were still uncertain. The first departure left Newport at 4.45am and the last service to Blaenavon was at 10.00pm. The last through train southbound to Newport left Blaenavon at 9.00pm. There were two further departures, one left at 10.00pm that terminated at Panteg and Griffithstown and a final departure 11.05pm that terminated at Cwmbran.

Sundays were a different matter with only one through train from Newport to Blaenavon at 6.15am, which arrived at 7.21am and formed the one through return journey, which departed at 7.30am. Other trains during the day operated a shorter service from Pontypool (Crane Street) to Newport at 9.35am and 9.45pm respectively and northbound services were at 7.45am, 8.50am and a final evening departure at 10.55pm but all these terminated at Pontypool (Crane Street).

Until the introduction of the DMU sets, steam hauled auto-trains comprising an 0-6-0 pannier tank, usually from Newport (Ebbw Junction) shed, with one or possibly two coaches being the norm. However the highlight of the day was known as the 'Hereford Stopper', which was the 5.34pm departure from Newport that usually featured a Castle or Hall class that called at all stations and arrived at Hereford at 7.15pm (weekdays) and 7.00pm (Saturdays only). This service used the Eastern Valley line as far as Panteg and Griffithstown and then branched right at Coed-y-Gric Junction to Pontypool Road. These services connected with through trains to Shrewsbury, Crewe and the North of England.

NEWPORT

Blaenavon Low Level
Cwmavon
Cwmffrwd Halt
Abersychan
Snatchwood Halt
Pontnewynydd
Pontypool (Crane Street)
Pontypool Blaendare Road
Panteg & Griffithstown
Sebastopol
Pontrhydyrun Halt
Upper Pontnewydd
Cwmbran
Llantarnam
Llantarnam Road
Ponthir
Caerleon
Mill Street
Maindee Junction
High Street
To Docks
To Severn
Tunnel Junction
NEWPORT

Our journey begins in Newport, an important town on the river Usk, which according to *Bradshaw's 1861 Handbook*, 'with the exception of the church, the town itself has no prepossessing attractions'. As the Industrial Revolution took off in Britain in the nineteenth century the south Wales valleys became key suppliers of coal and iron. The Monmouthshire Canal was opened in 1796 to capitalise on this growing trade and Newport and its docks grew rapidly as a result and became one of the largest towns in Wales and the focus for the expanding new industries.

High Street station had the benefit of having through roads, which allowed for the transit of freight from the coalfields and steel works without having to occupy platform space, which were used for the many passenger trains arriving and departing.

Taken on 24th July 1961 our picture shows ex-GWR 4200 class 2-8-0T No 4227 of 86A Newport (Ebbw Junction) shed passing eastbound through the station light engine whilst in the background another ex-GWR 4200 class 2-8-0T No 5224 of 86E Severn Tunnel Junction shed approaches the newly commissioned multi-aspect signal gantry, bunker first with a westbound freight train.

The *South Wales Pullman* was the premier express service running non-stop between London (Paddington) and Newport and on to Swansea. Here we see a fine view of ex-GWR 4073 Castle class 4-6-0 No 5051 *Earl Bathurst* an 87A Neath engine at the head of a rake of eight Pullman coaches having just arrived with the 9.55pm from Paddington to Swansea on 17th July 1961.

BR Standard class 9F 2-10-0 No 92220 appropriately named *Evening Star* was the last steam locomotive built by British Railways at Swindon on 18th March 1960 and allocated new to Cardiff (Canton) shed. It was painted in brunswick green a colour normally reserved for express passenger locomotives and is shown here with a freight train steaming through the centre road at Newport on 17th July 1961. It was withdrawn in March 1965 after less than five years in service and is now preserved on static display at the National Railway Museum, York.

This aerial shot shows the remains of
Newport Castle between the railway and
road bridges on the right hand bank of
the river Usk. Also shown is Mill Street
gas works and the MRCC line on the
right of the picture swinging underneath
the road crossing at the Old Green and
reappearing heading toward the docks
after passing Moderator Wharf sidings
on the left.

Three miles north of Newport and having crossed the river Usk at St. Julian's Bridge, we arrive at Caerleon where the Romans built their first settlement in 75AD; the station was opened in 1874 on the PCN line. There was a racecourse here where the Welsh Grand National was run for the one and only time in1948 when many thousands arrived by special excursion trains. The following year it was transferred to Chepstow racecourse where it has remained ever since.

Ex-GWR 6000 King class 4-6-0 No 6000 *King George V* the doyen of the class with a full head of steam approaches Caerleon on the 9th October 1971 hauling a rake of Pullman coaches on its return trip north to Hereford with a 'Return to Steam' special from Swindon.

The locomotive was named after the then monarch of the United Kingdom, King George V. Built at Swindon in 1927 and following a period of running-in the locomotive was shipped to the United States in August of that year to feature in the Baltimore & Ohio's centenary celebrations. During the celebrations, it was presented with a bell and a plaque and these are carried to this day.

The locomotive was officially preserved as part of the national collection and was restored to main line running order and located at the Bulmer's Railway Centre in Hereford. In 1971 it became the first locomotive to break the ban on steam traction which had been imposed by BR following the end of steam on the network in August 1968. Its restoration to main line running is often credited with opening the door for the return of steam to the UK.

A fine shot of Caerleon signal box with the cattle pens shown behind as ex-GWR 2-8-2T 7200 class No 7210 of 86G Pontypool Road shed heads north with a short freight on 8th August 1961. The signal box was closed on 20th August the same year.

Ex-GWR 4900 Hall class 4-6-0 No 4993 *Dalton Hall* an 85A Worcester engine steams through Caerleon with a southbound freight on Monday 28th August 1961.

Swindon built three-car cross-country units 50647, 59255 and 50696 form the 10.45am service from Cardiff (General) to Birmingham (Snow Hill) on Wednesday 7th June 1961 as it runs through Caerleon to its next call at Pontypool Road.

Ex-GWR 4900 Hall class 4-6-0 No 6919 *Tylney Hall* of 82A Bristol (Bath Road) shed passes through Caerleon with a Manchester to Plymouth train on 10th April 1959.

PONTHIR

The next station along the line at Ponthir opened in 1879. This is a mainly residential area that was established when a local brickworks using clay from a nearby quarry opened in the 1930s. Its only other claim to fame is that it was the first place in Britain where bacteria was used to treat sewage sludge in the nearby water treatment works.

The picture shows ex-GWR 4073 Castle class 4-6-0 No 5015 *Kingswear Castle* of 82A Bristol (Bath Road) shed leaving Ponthir with a down express for the west country in 1961.

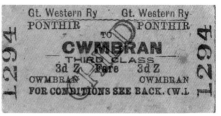

What appears to be an unidentified Saint class locomotive hauling a Hereford to Cardiff express passes through the station whilst passengers head for the footbridge to board a local northbound train.

LLANTARNAM

We now arrive at Llantarnam, the site of a Cistercian Abbey founded in 1179 the remains of which are incorporated into the current buildings of Llantarnam Abbey. There were two stations here, the first was opened on the original MRCC line and called Llantarnam Road using the accepted practice of naming stations 'Road' where they were some distance from population centres. This closed on 11th March 1880 following the opening of the second Llantarnam station on the PCN line when all passenger traffic was switched to Newport High Street. North of the station, the Eastern Valley line branched left at Llantarnam Junction, whilst the main Hereford line continued on to Pontypool Road.

In 1938 Weston opened their new factory, the home of the famous 'Wagon Wheel' and 'Jammy Dodger' biscuits. The factory was to provide employment for hundreds of workers in an area that was known as a 'distressed region' hit especially hard by the Depression. The site had a number of private sidings that have since been removed and is now owned by Burton's Biscuits and still in full production.

Such was the importance attached to the factory opening that the Weston Biscuit Special hauled by ex-GWR 4073 Castle class 4-6-0 No 5070 *Sir Daniel Gooch*, out-shopped from Swindon only a few months beforehand and allocated to Old Oak Common shed, hauled a special train and is seen awaiting departure from Paddington with 150 dignitaries on board. These included many business executives, amongst them company chairman, Garfield Weston, and former Canadian Prime Minister, Richard Bedford Bennett.

One of the services offered to customers by the GWR was farm movements and here we see one such move from Llantarnam to West Grinstead where a complete farm including livestock are loaded onto cattle wagons at Weston's private sidings with the family watching on 30th September 1947.

A mishap occurred at Llantarnam in the 1960s when a tank engine that was shunting on the private sidings of Weston Biscuits broke a coupling sending the guards van through the station buildings.

Ex-GWR 4-6-0 4900 Hall class
No 6946 *Heatherden Hall* of 86C
Cardiff (Canton) shed heads the 12.45pm
service from Birmingham (Snow Hill)
to Cardiff through Llantarnam on
10th June 1957. Westons can be seen
on the left of the picture.

The next station Cwmbran, originally spelt as Cwmbrain, was where the original MRCC line from Newport merged with the PCN line at Cwmbran Junction. The New Towns Act 1946 highlighted the need for post-war redevelopment and Cwmbran was the only one to be built in Wales. It was established in 1949 to provide new employment opportunities in the south eastern portion of the south Wales coalfield.

The first station in Cwmbran was opened in 1852 by the MRCC. Once the new PCN line was opened in 1878, a new station was built on a short connecting branch from Llantarnam Junction opening on 1 August 1880. This replaced the 1852 station. The current Cwmbran station, on the line from Newport to Hereford, is located north of the site of Llantarnam Junction and opened on 12th May 1986.

This picture shows part of the remains of the original MRCC station platform on the left hand side of the picture.

This August 1960 picture shows the original MRCC line to Newport docks merging with the Eastern Valley line at the rear of Cwmbran Junction signal box.

UPPER PONTNEWYDD

Opened on 1st July 1852 by the MRCC, the original station named Pontnewydd served an eighteenth century settlement that grew steadily with the rise in heavy industry such as coal, iron and tin plate. It has been recorded that the station was briefly known as Upper Cwmbran from 1st September until 4th November 1881, although this was never formally recognised and the station was renamed Upper Pontnewydd.

Pontnewydd Golf Club, first established in 1875, is reputedly the oldest such club in Wales.

PONTRHYDYRUN HALT

Approximately half way along the line we find Pontrhydyrun Halt. The station here was first opened in 1873 as Pontrhydyrun and closed in 1917. Pontrhydyrun Halt was opened on 17th July 1933 a quarter of a mile south of the site of the original station.

On Thursday 29th July 1982, the stone bridge that carried the original Eastern Valley line was the scene of carnage when a double-decker bus owned by the National Welsh Omnibus Company had its roof completely sliced off killing six people and seriously injuring a further eight. The bus was on a day trip to Porthcawl, when the driver apparently took a wrong turn, which resulted in the crash. Following the accident investigation it was revealed that there had been four previous bridge strikes over the past three years. The bridge was demolished soon afterwards.

We next arrive at Sebastopol, once a small village that has now been encompassed by nearby Panteg. The village was named in honour of the Crimean city of Sevastopol although there were only basic facilities here as seen from the weed and grass strewn platforms. The original station was named as Sebastopol and opened in December 1875 but was later renamed Panteg and closed in July 1880. In 1928 another station was opened on the Eastern Valley line called Sebastopol.

The picture shows ex-GWR 5700 class 0-6-0PT No 8716 of 86G Pontypool Road shed passing through the station with a short train of mineral wagons.

PANTEG & GRIFFITHSTOWN

Our next station is Panteg & Griffithstown. There was a large steelworks established here in 1873 to produce rails for export to India and a number of innovative products such as the first full production of stainless steel outside of Sheffield in 1944; the works closed in 2004.

The station, Panteg, was originally opened in 1880 on the MRCC line and was re-named as Panteg and Griffithstown in 1898 in honour of the first station master at Pontypool Road, Henry Griffiths.

This aerial view illustrates the extent of the layout of Panteg Steelworks and its sidings showing the main north and west line on the left and the Eastern Valley line on the right of the picture. The staggered platforms are shown in the foreground and just beyond the footbridge at the bottom of the picture the line swings right at Coed-y-Gric Junction to join the NA&HR towards Pontypool Road.

This picture shows ex-GWR 5600 class
0-6-2T No 6675 of 86G Pontypool Road
shed passing through the station with an
empty coaching stock working.

Another view of the station with ex-GWR 5700 class 0-6-0-PT No 5756 of 86G Pontypool Road shed running southbound with a coal train on 29th September 1960.

This picture shows the track layout at Coed-y-Gric Junction looking north with the line diverging to the right leading toward Pontypool Road and the north and west route to Hereford. The Eastern Valley line carries straight on and Panteg and Coed-y-Gric Junction signal box can be seen in the centre of the picture.

This was little more than a wayside halt with basic facilities opened in 1928, built at the foot of a long hill leading up to Jones West Monmouth School, which was founded in 1898 by William Jones a London haberdasher. It served the local communities of Pontymoile and Cwmynyscoy.

Standing in the platform bunker first with a morning northbound service in 1962 is an unidentified Hawksworth 9400 class 0-6-0PT.

Seen in the platform is an unidentified Derby built DMU on a Blaenavon to Newport service.

Pontypool has a notable history as one of the earliest industrial towns in Wales. It was served by four stations with two on the Taff Vale Extension line to Quaker's Yard, namely Pontypool Road and Clarence Street, which was originally called Pontypool Town, and Blaendare Road and Crane Street. This was first opened in 1854 as Pontypool, the terminus of the MRCC line to Newport. In 1881 the station became known as Crane Street to distinguish it from the other stations in the town.

Pontypool was well known for its rugby club, which was founded in 1870 and immortalised in song by Welsh artist Max Boyce as *The Pontypool Front Row*.

Soldiers of the 2nd Battalion, The Monmouthshire Regiment, awaiting departure for the Front at the outbreak of World War One in August 1914.

An unidentified ex-GWR 5600 class 0-6-2T arrives at the station on a wet day in 1960.

Between Pontypool Crane Street and Pontnewynydd, the line diverged to the left at Trevethin Junction as shown in the picture opposite.

This line served a number of unstaffed wayside halts as it climbed away to join the London & North Western Railway 'top line' at Blaenavon High Level. The line then continued towards Brynmawr where it met with the Abergavenny to Merthyr line (see *Lost Lines of Wales – The Heads of the Valleys Line*) and the Western Valley line (see *Lost Lines of Wales – Monmouthshire Western Valley*).

The line was closed to passengers on 5th May 1941 as a wartime economy measure although the line itself remained open for coal traffic until the closure of the Big Pit in 1980.

PONTNEWYNYDD

This station was opened in 1854. The galvanizing works shown in the background employed many workers and once produced the corrugated iron Anderson air raid shelter used during the Second World War.

We next arrive at Snatchwood Halt, which had staggered platforms with basic facilities. It was opened on 13th July 1912 to serve local collieries and a brickworks and, sometime later, Snatchwood Hospital. Shown here during the bleak winter of 1947, the station closed on 5th October 1953.

ABERSYCHAN LOW LEVEL

Not to be confused with the other station on the former LNWR line to Blaenavon High Level, which was known as Abersychan and Talywain, we now pull in to Abersychan. The suffix 'Low Level' was added to the Eastern Valley station in 1885 and was well used by pupils attending the local grammar school where former Home Secretary Roy Jenkins was once a pupil.

School's out and it is time to go home! Pupils from the local grammar school await the arrival of the 3.54pm service to Newport as they break for the Whitsun holiday on 19th May 1961, although the driver appears to have forgotten to change the destination blind that reads Cardiff.

Ex-GWR 6400 class 0-6-0PT No 6403 of 86G Pontypool Road shed arrives at the station with the 4.04pm service to Blaenavon on 8th June 1957.

This was another station on the line that had staggered platforms.

CWMFFRWD HALT

Arriving at Cwmffrwd and the end of the double track from Newport. The station was opened in 1912 and should not be confused with Cwmffrwdoer Halt, which opened at the same time on the LNWR line to Blaenavon High Level. Hawksworth designed 9400 class 0-6-0PT No 8480 of 87A Neath shed departs with a northbound passenger train with the signalman handing the token to the driver as the line to Blaenavon was single track from here. The locomotive was withdrawn in July 1964 after only 12 years in service.

CWMAVON (MON) HALT

Our next stop is Cwmavon. This was opened after the construction of the Eastern Valley section of the MRCC in 1854. The line was known as the low level railway to distinguish it from the LNWR Blaenavon to Brynmawr branch line, which opened in 1868 further uphill on the west side of the valley. The station was classed as a Halt from 8th June 1953. The addition of (Mon) was added to timetables to avoid confusion with Cwmavon in the Afan Valley of the now Neath Port Talbot County Borough.

Ex-GWR 5700 class 0-6-0PT No 5752 arrives with the 2.46pm service to Newport on 8th June 1957. Withdrawn in 1960 it was then transferred to London Transport as L91 working out of Neasden depot.

A special train from Blaenavon to Porthcawl carrying passengers on their way to view a fireworks spectacular at Coney Beach Funfair is seen arriving at the station in September 1961.

BLAENAVON LOW LEVEL

Our final station at the end of the line is Blaenavon. The town lies at the source of the Afon Llwyd (grey river) and by 1800 Blaenavon Ironworks contributed to south Wales becoming the foremost iron producing region in the world; the area is now a UNESCO World Heritage site.

The station opened in 1854 and the suffix Low Level was added in 1950. It closed to passenger traffic from 30th April 1962.

On the 29th March 1948 with the engine still carrying its GWR number on the buffer beam ex-GWR 5700 class 0-6-0PT No 3634 of 86A Newport (Ebbw Junction) shed is shown on the 1.32pm service to Newport.

In February 2001 a team of archaeologists from Channel 4 television attempted to uncover the world's first railway viaduct built here in 1790, but due to safety reasons the project was eventually abandoned.

Awaiting departure with the 10.00am to Newport is a Derby built DMU during the last days of service in 1962.

WAY OUT

S·L·S
SPECIAL
6656

Within a week of closure the first enthusiasts' special arrived at Blaenavon. Ex-GWR 5600 class 0-6-2T No 6656 of 86A Newport (Ebbw Junction) shed is seen with a Stephenson Locomotive Society rail tour on 6th May 1962.